GOD'S AMAZING CREATURES

BY

STANLEY F BOTTEN

PREFACE. God's Amazing Creatures is a book that has been compiled to show the amazing creatures that inhabit our earth, and their place in the echo system and how they all fit into the system. The author is an amateur photographer who has taken pictures of animals over a period of 40 years. The advances in digital cameras and the ease of producing good pictures has made it relatively easy for the amateur photographer to produce.

Most of these pictures have been taken in the reserves in South Africa and use these to promote the grandeur of our almighty Father the one and only God who created these beautiful majestic creatures both great and small.

- The equipment used for the technical minded is the pictures were taken with the new Canon D70 Rebel XT Digital camera and a 70 to 300 mm telephoto lens with image Stabilizer, and the pictures have been processed with CS5 Photo shop.

This book is in response to the request from many who have heard and seen my presentations.

- Most of the pictures used in this book where taken during visits to that amazing private game park Ingwelala on the border of the Kruger National Park.

- We open with a picture taken on the South Coast of Natal located on the eastern shore of southern Africa at a holiday resort known as San Lameer.

An amazing fact of nature is that God made the creatures and the feeding habits to suit the environment, for example the tall Giraffe feed on the leaves on the tops of the trees and the Buffalo, the Impala and the other Antelopes feed on the grass on the ground level. Animals like the Elephant feed at a higher level than the Impala.

When we study nature and the environment, how can we question whether God made the world and all that is in it. His mighty hand is on everything and we all have a place from the smallest insect to the mighty Elephant.

TABLE OF CONTENTS.

Pictures	Description.	Page
1	The waves and beaches	4
2	Sand Crab	5
3	Dung Beetle	6
4	African Butterfly	7
5	Lizard Eating a spider	8
6	African Spider	9
7	Scorpion	10
8	Grass Hopper	11
9	Ermine Crested Bee Eater	12
10	Yellow Throated Bee Eater	13
11	Common Bee Eater	14
12	Common Hornbill	15
13	Crested Barbet	16
14	Lilac Breasted Roller	17
15	Lilac Breasted Roller picture 2	18
16	Young Lilac Breasted Roller	19
17	Blue King Fisher	20
18	Grey Lowrie	21
19	Franklin Partridge	22
20	Franklin Partridge Camouflage	23
21	Great White Stork	24
22	Saddle Billed Stork	25
23	Horned Owl	26
24	Marshall Eagle standing	27
25	Marshall Eagle in Flight	28
26	Marshall Eagle in thought	29
27	Cape Vulture on branch	30
28	Cape Vultures feeding	31
29	Red Billed Hornbill	32
30	Warthog Sow with litter	33
31	Male African Warthog	34
32	Male Kudu Bull Antelope	35
33	Female Doe Kudu	36
34	Male Impala Antelope	37
35	Female Doe Impala prancing	38
36	Male Waterbuck	39
37	Blue Wilderbees	40
38	Nyala Does	41
39	Male Bull Nyala antelope	42
40	Male Cape Buffalo Bull	43
41	Small herd of Buffalo drinking	44
42	Cape Buffalo rolling in the mud	45
43	Male Giraffe	46
44	Small Herd of Elephants with young	47
45	Old Female Elephant	48
46	Mature Bull Elephant	49
47	Elephant viewing from land rover	50
48	African Blue Rhino	51
49	Burchell Zebra	52
50	Two Male Lions	53
51	Male lion scarred face	54
52	Young Lion Feeding	55
53	African Leopard	56
54	African leopard with kill in tree	57

PICTURE 1. This picture shows the majestic waves and the storm on the horizon this is clear evidence of the Glory of God.

PICTURE 2. The lowly sand crab that is found on all the beaches of Africa. If you sit quiet they will come out of their burrow. God made them large He made them small He made them one and all.

PICTURE 3. The fascinating Lowly Dung Beetle, who gathers the dung from the larger animals such as the Buffalo and the Elephant and creates a ball. The male will gather the dung form a ball and roll this to a suitable location, the female seen on top of the ball will lay her eggs inside. The young on hatching will feed on the dung until ready to do their part in the evolution of life.

PICTURE 4. The beautiful African Butterfly has it's part to play by gathering the nectar from the flowers and at the same time pollinating the flowers so that the seeds will form.

PICTURE 5. Meanwhile the small predators such as we see here the common Lizard has found his first meal a spider.

PICTURE 6. This spider escaped and is now weaving and constructing his web to catch the flying insects for his next meal.

PICTURE 7. There are a number of Scorpions species that inhabit the earth some a more poisonous than others and can grow up to 10 inches long. The poisonous types have large thick tails and small pincers as they use their poison to subdue their prey. The lesser poisonous types have larger pincers and a thin tail. However the sting is

PICTURE 8. This colorful Grass Hopper can grow up to 3 inches in length and can do a lot of damage to crops and grass fields. But unlike the it's cousin the Locust is seldom found in swarms that can clear a field of any vegetation in minutes, the size of the swarms can be several thousand locust at any one time

PICTURE 9. There are over 200 species of birds in Africa and is always a delight to see with their colorful plumage. This bird is an Ermine chested Bee eater. Whose main diet are bees. Unlike most birds it makes its nest in the form of a small tunnel in the side embankment of the river bed

PICTURE 10. This is the Yellow throated Bee Eater slightly smaller than the previous one

PICTURE 11. In this picture we see the common Bee eater with a Bee in its beak sitting on a Telephone cable.

PICTURE 12. This is a picture of the common African Hornbill. A very interesting bird sometimes referred to as the clown of the bush. It's breeding habits are very interesting the male bird will find a suitable hole in a tree and the female will enter and the male will take clay and close the entrance so that only her beak is clear. She will then shed all her feathers and line the nest using this and will stay there for the full duration of the egg laying, hatching and rearing of the chicks. The male will feed them all until they are ready to leave the nest.

PICTURE 13. The Crested Barbet is a small colorful bird often found in the back garden of homes of people who have bird feeders.

PICTURE 14. This beautiful bird is shy and not easily photographed you need a good telephoto lens to capture a good picture. It is known as the Lilac Breasted Roller. The Afrikaans name for this bird is very descriptive Trou Poe. Translated. The wedding peacock. And is found mainly in the bush veld

PICTURE 15. Another view of the Lilac Breasted Roller showing the chest color that gives it it's name.

PICTURE 16. A young Lilac Breasted Roller that has not yet developed its full colors.

PICTURE 17.A picture of the strikingly beautiful Blue King Fisher, who will sit on a branch overlooking a stream and will on seeing a small fish will dive down and catch the unwary fish.

PICTURE 18. The Grey Lowrie. This is a medium sized bird that is commonly called the GO AWAY bird. It gets this name from the call it makes that sounds like GO AWAY. It uses this cry as an alarm and is hated by hunters as it will wait until the hunter is ready to shoot and then will make this call, chasing the animal away

PICTURE 19. The Franklin Partridge this bird is very common in Africa and is hunted by both

PICTURE 20. In this picture the Franklin Partridge coloring blends very well with the back ground and is a perfect example of natures camouflage.

PICTURE 21. The Great White Stork coming in for a landing on its nest constructed of twigs this bird grows to about 4 feet high and the myth exists that this is the stork that brings the babies. They migrate from the northern Europe way down to Africa.

PICTURE 22. The Saddle Billed Stork in this picture is now on the endangered list and protected people who spot this bird are asked to report the time date and location to the Park Authorities. It grows as large as 4 feet high.

PICTURE 23. The Horned Owl the silent predatory bird that makes no sound as it flies through the air. Natur
has designed the feathers so that they do not make a sound as the owl flies. This allows the Owl to bounce on
the small rodents as they scurry through the grass looking for food.

26

PICTURE 24. The majestic Marshall Eagle surveying the land always on the lookout for small mammals. Its sharp beak and claws are their weapons.

PICTURE 25. The Marshall Eagle in flight with a small mammal in its claws

CTURE 26. Marshal Eagle deep in thought "How did I miss that rabbit"

PICTURE 27. The Cape Vulture they are the sanitary cleaners of Africa and feed mainly on dead animals eating all the left over's from the large predators.

PICTURE 28. This pictures shows the Cape Vultures feed on an animal carcass

PICTURE 29. The Red Billed Horn bill, this bird feeds on grubs and worms found in the bark of a tree

PICTURE 30. African Warthog sow with a litter of piglets foraging for food.

PICTURE 31. The Male African Warthog from the size of his tusks a very mature male.

PICTURE 32. The majestic Kudu Bull regarded as the king of the African Antelopes with a red beaked Oxpecker on its back. The Oxpecker is the friend of all the herbivores as it feeds on all the parasites that bother them. The age of the Kudu is gauged by the number of curls in the horns a fully developed mature bull will have three curls and will weigh up to 1,600 lbs.

PICTURE 33. The Kudu Doe is smaller and will have no horns.

PICTURE 34. The male Impala seen here about to drink is the main source of food for the Leopard and will be found in small herds of up to 50 doe and one male. On the outskirts of the herd will be the less mature male antelopes, awaiting their chance to take over the herd

PICTURE 35. A mature female Doe Impala prancing along. The Impala are very agile and will jump as high as 15 feet.

ICTURE 36. A male Water Buck note the distinctive marking especially around the tail. This animal is found mostly close to water

PICTURE 37. An animal that is found on the open grass lands known as the Blue Wilderbees a derivative from the early Dutch settlers that called it this as it reminded them of wild cattle. Te lions will often select these as their prey.

PICTURE 38. The dainty shy Nyala doe's feeding on the fresh green grass.

PICTURE 39. The male (Bull) Nyala antelope much smaller than the Kudu but very attractive.

PICTURE 40. A fully grown large Cape Buffalo. This animal is classed as one of the big five most aggressive animals found in Africa. If wounded is known to lay an ambush for the Hunter.

PICTURE 41. A small herd of Cape Buffalo drinking water, herds as large as one thousand are now found in the Kruger Game Reserve.

PICTURE 42. A Cape Buffalo rolling in the mud to put a layer of mud to keep the parasites away and as a sun screen. Copper Tone Sun Tan Lotion is not readily available in the bush.

PICTURE 43. A male Giraffe browsing and feeding on the upper leaves of an acacia tree.

PICTURE 44. A small Herd of Elephants with young digging in the dry river bed for water. Note that the young elephants are in the middle and the older mature elephants are outside providing protection.

PICTURE 45. An older female Elephant note how small the tusks are, but be careful she will be very short tempered

PICTURE 46. A mature Bull Elephant who is drinking at the water's edge. A very Majestic and wonderful creature.

PICTURE 47. Close but not too close, Elephants must be treated with respect at all times.

PICTURE 48. The African Blue Rhino, an animal that also needs to be respected although short sited has a tremendous sense of smell

PICTURE 49. The Burchel Zebra. It is easy to understand how the stripes and the grouping will confuse the Lion

PICTURE 50. Two Male Lions resting in the shade of a tree during the heat of the day. Truly the King of the beasts.

PICTURE 51. Scarface voicing his domination of the area. It is suspected that he had been in a fight with the head of a pride of Lions in the area.

PICTURE 52. A young Lion Feeding on a Zebra that they had killed that day

PICTURE 53. The African Leopard a truly Beautiful creature with distinct markings, but a known killer who will kill without provocation.

PICTURE 54. The African Leopard will kill its prey and then at its leisure feed, here we see it taking a nap after feeding

PICTURE 55. The beautiful African sunset over the African bush